# *A little faith, hope and love*

# *Poetry by, Rosalind M Patton*

## Contents

# <u>Introduction</u>

Hi and thank you for picking up my little book, this has been a labour of love. A lot of back and fourths, stops and starts. I have always had difficulty finishing this because I never thought it would be good enough to read. While this was the kind of person I was, I have always been a thinker, a feeler, a listener and an observer of the world and I thought "Where is the harm in sharing what one loves to do?"

The collection I have chosen to include are random in their appearance. Each poem was provoked by comment, a thought, and an experience and even influenced by other readings and speeches.

Everything around us is an experience. We are like children, yet we don't embrace experiences like them all the time. They hear a new word and they are intrigued. They want to know more, they want to learn, they are curious. As an adult when we hear something new we don't want to admit we lack an understanding. Therefore, we don't learn, we don't get curious and we don't grow to our full potential.

Our potential is limitless. It is ourselves that installs our potential. I have an approach to life that anyone can do anything. The reason I say that is because I have had many jobs over the years, all of which I didn't know I could do until I did them. Growing is endless. Adding strings to your bow doesn't mean you can't settle on anything in life, it just means you have a natural curiosity to explore new things and not afraid to take chances on change.

I have completed also so many courses and none of them kept my interest for any great length of time. That said, I have done them. I'm not sorry I took a chance. It didn't turn out to be right choice for me but I still experienced something new and at that time I enjoyed it. Each new topic broadened me in some ways.

All that said the one thing I never really explored was the one thing I feared and loved the most which was writing. I would think "Who wants to read what you have written?".

Again I say this because I attempted my GCSE English three times so I'm clearly not that great at it or I would have got it first time, right? Wrong. Looking back, I should have been looking at it in the sense that it may have took me three attempts to get my English GCSE but I got it. I stuck it out because I knew I needed it in life. That's called determination. I was a slow reader so I wouldn't read books. I would read or buy foot notes so I could hold a conversation on a book of topic.

It wasn't until later in life I would admit I'd never read a book from start to finish all in one go, like this book of my own. I would start and stop and start and stop again. I could never understand why I didn't have the same passion for books which others had yet I loved to write. I always thought I had a lack of understanding or short attention span.

Again, only recently I discovered what it was. I had more of an affinity with poetry, short stories and real life readings and events. I may have struggled to read books from start to finish but have you ever read the quote from The Odyssey by Homer? "Of all the creatures that breathe and move upon the earth, nothing is bred that is weaker than man" or the quote by Sylvia Plath "If you expect nothing from anybody, you are never disappointed". We all have our things in life which we have great connections with. Mine tends to be with poetry, real life and observations.

I would encourage those who don't have a connection with a novel or any book to understand that you don't have to. I ask you this, do you read magazines of interest? Do you read newspapers from start to finish? do you read social media and articles which draw your attention? If so then you are a reader, a learner and an educated mind.

Which leads me back to why I have chosen to publish my own book of poetry because all reading is good reading to the reader and the one who connects with it. If I can get you to connect or ever identify with even one of my poems within this book then to me I have accomplished what I set out to do.

Poetry to me is an experience and then words carefully placed in particular order to provoke the mind to think, feel and visualise. A poem can encourage the mind to create a story. Short stories and books get the same desired out come as reading a poem. The difference is a poem will stick with you, it will keep provoking thought each time you read or recite it.

Yes, a poet has written with influence and reasoning but to me all is open to interpretation unless you have a direct conversation with the writer. Take this quote/poem for example:

"Out beyond ideas
 of wrongdoing and rightdoing
there is a field, I will meet you there." Jelaluddin Rumi, 13th Century.

This is a poem by poet and philosopher by the name of Rumi wrote in the 13th Century and it is still as relevant now as it was over 600 years ago.

I interpret this as, forget the ideals of perfect life and being good and the pressures of always doing the right thing along with the accidents of doing the wrong thing and come to a place where you can't offend and you can't do any wrong, you just simply have to be you completely unapologetically you. Sit in that field and answer to no one but yourself. I personally can't think of anything more ideal. I'm sure other theorists and poets have their own ideology of what this poem means but to me this is how I see it.

And this is what I encourage any reader to do with my writings. See it and interrupt it as you will. If you want my explanation on the writings, then make contact with me. Let's see if we think the same.

## <u>Special dedication</u>

My grandmother never got her recognition for being a writer. My grandmother also loved to recite poetry. She believed that intelligence wasn't smart. I have lived with this comment in my head my entire life ever since my mum told me of it. And it only echoes what I have said above. We all connect with things differently. Without her love of poetry and literature I may never have realised mine. It was clearly in me and inherited in some way. It was in my DNA. My grandmother was never published. She was a silent introverted beauty with beautiful words within her.

So, now I would like to introduce Rosetta Coyle to the world and share two of her poems. They have been provided by her daughters, my mum Helen (Sweet Blue Bell) and my godmother Mary (Little Birds).

## <u>Little birds</u>

I asked him wither the birds do fly?
In the woods and high in the sky?
Some go off to foreign clime and come back here in
the summer time.

These are the little birds up in the tree born,
In the little nest their mother made from grass, twigs
and thorn!

She fed them on grubs and worms she picked them
from the earth below,

Until their little wing grew strong, and they had to go.

The robin is my favorite with breast of ruby red,
because he is so gentle

I picked him instead.

All the other birdies have coarser beaks than he.
And peck you if you catch them till your sore as sore
can be!

*<u>Written by Rosetta Coyle</u>*

## Sweet Blue bell

I was going to school one day
I smelt the smell of the new moon hay
All in the meadow there beside the purlin stream
And on that stream, beside the well I smelt the smell
Of the sweet blue bell.

*Written by Rosetta Coyle*

## Dedications

My family. My absolute back bone. They are and always will be the loves of my life. I could never have a more secure and loving family. My sisters and brother have been pillars in my life. My sibling are the most kind hearted people I will ever know in my life. They have helped me more times than I can count. There are no such thing as hard times when you have family like mine around you. Dedicating this book to them is one of the easiest decision I have ever had to make. Thank you.

I have to say huge thank you to my Aunt Mary who helped with the editing and encouraged my writing. When I left my works in her hands she said she was "delighted and honored" that I trusted her with them. All I can say is, it was I who was delighted and honored that she would graciously review them. Mary also hand wrote grannies poem that are seen within the book. Another unrecognised talent. I guess the apple didn't fall to far from grandmothers' tree. Thank you Mary.

A man who came into my life in the summer of my years was Brian Hasson Jr. He has helped my confidence in un-describable ways. He has encouraged me, educated me and given me a true friend for life. If ever there was a truer gentle man put on this earth they must meet Brain Hasson Jr. A gentleman with extreme talent and his talent he shares freely at no cost or gain. I have learnt a lot from this beautiful soul. Thank you.

Colleen Brown, without whom the book may not have seen the light of day. She encouraged me in so many ways. It was her that gave me the push on a daily basis to complete this book. She encouraged me to push past my fear, put this out into the world and see what happens. I am truly grateful that she could see what could be done. Thank you.

Last but never least my mum. The undiscovered lady. My mum has the most beautiful soul. She is kind, loving, caring and funny. She is beautiful inside and out. A woman who I try to reflect myself on. Whose strength has always amazed me. No-one would ever know the difficult times my mum has been through because she is internally strong. I always remember my mum getting up and ready every day. She was always beautifully dressed with her hair and make-up done. On difficult days when I was younger I would think "Why does she bother?". Mum then told me one day when I was having my own difficulties, "No one needs to know your struggling. There will be days you struggle and there will be days you don't. People don't need to know. Keep your head high and all will pass. Keep your faith and you will be glad you always put your best foot forward."

She has an overwhelming amount of pride and she is strength. As a family we have been through some tough times. Raring four children on her own with no help made her wonder woman to me. Unable to work until we were able to fend for ourselves, she did a blinding job on very little. Never was our bellies hungry. Never were our clothes grubby or dirty. Never did we feel unloved or a burden. Never did I feel like we had very little because we had love in our hearts that was put there by our mother. We were as rich as rich could be. My mum was the Queen of mothers in my eyes. No education can teach what she gave us. Pure, unselfish, unconditional love. Thank you mum for being in my life and giving me my strength.

## Blood line

Family by definition. Family by blood. The good and the bad, happy and the sad. You understand and accept it all because you are one for all. Life beyond your mothers' door to your front door still holds a direct line. Be far or near, the connection is clear. The door you call your own opens for many and links to more.

Your door shares a resemblance to your mothers' door as does your sisters and brothers. Things we inherited we take through our own doors, that direct line from your mothers to yours holds an undeniable and undefinable link. One must think do I do what I do behind my door because this is how I do it? If so, then why when I go to a brothers, a sister, an aunt, a cousin, a niece or a nephews' door do I find myself in familiar surroundings?

No two homes the same, I cannot lie, but the link from, grandmothers to mothers to mine to yours each have a piece of home with them which helps to make my home. The direct line I cannot deny.

## <u>Welcoming Fire</u>

The light and heat from an open fire an all too welcoming beautiful sight. Warming a room and those within that room. From admiring the glow to the being emerged in the hot lava like coal. Flames burned the flesh, the heat fusing and shrinking the skin like the bones had become too large for the skin, a feeling like you had put on a glove which was too small for wearing, screams I can't remember, pain I don't believe I felt. Anguished loved ones, guilt, anxiety but no one at fault.

A child's hand disfigured by something so welcoming and warming but never meant for flesh to touch. A mother's faith, prayer, love and belief that the child could be healed was thought not to be enough, until one day it was enough.

The child's hand healed, a healing so unbelievable that no one to believe her story as an adult that she had fallen into a welcoming fire landing on hot lava like coal. A mother's faith, prayer, love and belief not to be questioned when power of faith is stronger than the flames of a fire.

## <u>Inherited</u>

Kinder spirts of a different time, of a different generation. Similar likes, years apart, similar interests' worlds' apart, similar attitudes and talents life times apart. We parted ways before our ways could have been compared. T'was not till later in life one would try to reconnect with your interests, your attitude and talent. Realise something you never had time to realise.

Life took you away from your passion, your calling your unrealised and undiscovered dexterity. Life gave you to us, your line, your life gave us memories and nostalgia. Your talent didn't skip beyond your line. The line exists because of you and the talents inherited come from you.

## Wasn't my tale to tell

I ran through an alley I was not allowed to be in, I passed playing children with no due regard for safety, no fear of injury. Down I ran in white patient shoes below the knee dress and cardigan over my arms.

I ran to tell a tale that wasn't mine to tell. You weren't allowed in that alley although I did not see my own disobedience only that of yours. I saw a defiance in you I did not see in me. So I ran to tell a tale that was not mine to tell. A tale that almost cost me my life, what a strife my family would have had to bare.

I reached my destination, your destination called home all to tell a tale that was not mine to tell. I reached your door and knocked so urgently with no due regard that I was almost killed by a bus. The door opens without any acknowledgement I told a tale that was not mine to tell. I shouted "your son is in an alley he's not allowed in". For telling a tale that wasn't mine to tell I learnt a lesson well.

## <u>Broken Biscuits</u>

Mum made raring her herd look easy with very little. Broken biscuits and dark lights were the best of nights. We would play in the grass all day, we come to the dinner table covered in the mud from the field and the scent of the grass we were rolling in. washed and ready for the next day, our bellies full, we cosy down with the lights dark and broken biscuits. We were not of monetary wealth, with the broken biscuits came the treats of sugar pieces. "Can I have a treat" we would ask to which we were never answered no. We were rich we had broken biscuits, sugar pieces and bellies full.

## <u>Tethered</u>

I never knew what tethered meant till I tethered with you. All thoughts, feeling, seeing, believing all came with a unison thought of; are you thinking the same? Do you react in the same pain? Same happiness, the same frustration.

We tethered before we met. A force which didn't come from out of the blue. It built until our paths were ready to and knew what to do. Ready to walk side by side but not at the same stride. Our strides are what brought us together, growing in each others learnings, leaning in each others growth. Watching, fighting, and colliding until we found a stride that still allows us to walk the path together but in our own beat with our own feet.

We tethered because we out weathered the weather. The bad storm we sat in we then aligned in.

We stride in what looks like different destinations to only arrive where we were meant to be. Side by side, yet still in our own stride.

We'll walk many a path like the ones we weathered but we will remain tethered.

## <u>My Right</u>

I had a fight, it was my right, do me wrong, shame on you. If I do me wrong shame on me. Courage from within, from where you have been to where you need to be.

You thought you could do me wrong, I told you to sail along, you didn't hear my plea so I had to make you heed. I took courage from your ignorance, you wanted to provoke fear, uncertainty and doubt. Don't you know we are cut from the same cloth? If you can hold form to do me wrong, I can hold form to do me right. You did me wrong shame on you! I stepped up to fight my fight, I did me right.

## <u>Dark Alley</u>

An alley full of light never felt so dark in the day until the day fear over comes. Fear clouds the light, when there are no glimpses of a shine, no brightness in the sky only darkness and fear, the unthinkable becomes a reality, a reality too much to bear, that the mind becomes numb and builds a darkness and a lightless wall around the fear until many a year when all becomes too much to bear. To build a wall around a trauma is to build a wall to protect the traumatisers, deal with the fear be free beyond the wall built to keep you in the darkness. No greater sight than the light beyond the dark.

## <u>Resemblance</u>

I love my mums' funny little moments, while she is looking at me thinking I'm strange, she's ignoring the fact that the apple may not have fallen far from her tree. I see me in her and I wonder does she see only the resemblance on the outside rather than the within me?

## <u>Clarity of the senses</u>

I see with clarity. I hear pitch perfectly. I smell as though I am in the garden from which you grew. I touch with every nerve experiencing an awakening. I taste every bite like it is my first. With all my senses working in perfect sync I am stimulated by a higher awakening and spiritual aligning, I enjoy each of these gifts with sincere appreciation.

Although to lose sight would only enhance what I hear. To lose hearing only enhances what I see. To lose smell and taste would only make me more curious about touch. I feel extreme gratitude for the senses I have and great respect for those with senses of a higher stimulant.

## Untouched Nature

The crisp air, the bright sun, the way I am wrapped up one would think it was too cold to embrace the air.

Oh to touch the leaves with my bare hand and not with synthetic ones I have become accustomed to.

Oh to breathe in the crisp air and not the fabric over my mouth and nose to protect me from the unknown and the what if.

I walk through the beautiful green land, the sun doing as it does, the air nipping the skin which is bare.

Nature doing what nature does, springing forward and blossoming.

The birds around me picking up branches and bark before my feet making a home for their fleet.

While I walk to my place of work afraid to speak, afraid to breathe without the protection of fabric on my face.

I walk home, I enjoy the sun, the air and the visual effects of the true beauty of nature.

Knowing how I took this for granted before the mask was introduced for protection.

This will only be short term, nature permanent.

When the time comes again I will walk through the green land with my bare hands touching the beauty, I will walk with no fabric over my mouth and nose and breathe in the true freshness,

I will appreciate what I once took for granted

## <u>Learn from your winter</u>

Winter never follows winter. The mind knows that something must always follow. Winter will never follow with another winter. Summer will never follow with another summer. The winter you are in will follow with spring. The difficult time you experience is what you have to weather before you arrive in a new season. Winter will never follow winter. Bad times will not follow more bad times. What has come must also go, experience allows us to grow and sow.

Winter will never follow winter. Learn now in your winter, what you will take into your summer. Leave the unwanted difficulty in the winter, prepare for the season of new, the season of spring then summer. Always know that winter will never follow another winter, it must come to pass, the now you are now in, must come to pass.

## A walk with nature

Nature took me by the hand today. The sun blinded my step, the cold cleansed my cheeks, the earth grounded me. The cool breeze made my head and thoughts clearer. My hands tingled with cold my toes numb, I couldn't have been anymore awake or aware as I seen my breath in the air, I paid more attention to the natural colours around me, each bark a different shade of brown from the last. Each tree different from the last some naked from the autumn fall, some blooming all year round.

I said hello to people whose breath I could see in the cold air with mine. Yet when we made eye contact it was the warmest of hellos. Nature earths us all. Nature is beautiful to the eye, and to the touch and to the person exploring.

## <u>All my senses</u>

I see without looking,

I feel without touching,

I hear without listening

I smell things without knowing what's there.

I taste things as though I heard the food growing, as if I've seen where it came from as if I heard the influences which help with its creation and as though I smell the aroma that discreetly fills the air. I have awakened the senses to new heights.

See without looking

Feel without touching

Hear without listening

Taste and smell things as though you were there.

## <u>Dark and lonely waters</u>

The town I love so well, polluted by choppers in the air, they swarm and hover over the dark and lonely grey polluted waters.

Polluted by trash and now it may seem many a life. Alarming to know how low one must go to throw their life away into the unwelcoming waters.

The water which looks so appealing like a song bird singing high. How that water must sound to the destitute in life.

Why they can't hear the song bird of life which sings for them to be free. Free from the things they cannot deal with and why they feel, the only way to deal is to NOT deal.

Two songbirds of life, one that gives us a false calm, the other lets us feel the warmth of a hand, a voice a kind tone to not feel alone.

A kind tone represents so much more than those who don't see the struggle could know.

To those who choose to deal by not dealing chose peace in the tormented mind.

Those who chose to deal in the real, chose a kind tone and the unknown.

## <u>Free is the soul</u>

Free is the soul. Free is the soul to wander and dream when it is absent from the body. Free is the soul to dream beyond the veil of sleep and wake. Free is the soul to dream up such things we only dare to imagine in the wake of day.

Why do we prefer to dream when we sleep? Are we so naive and unsure that we don't realise that dreams are meant for reality? Free is the soul to wander in the veiled reality of sleep, afraid to wake in the wake of reality that a dream is just dream. Or is it?

## **<u>Expressed sorrow</u>**

Sorrow must be expressed, let it out, feel the pain which causes the pain. Only then will you know how to heal. Understand and accept the sorrow which floods your heart and mind. Allow it to flow so you can grow. Allow it to flow, it will be easier to let it go. As obvious as the sun is to shine, sorrow will also have its place in time, time after time. Just as the sun will continue to shine sorrow will continue to heal.

## Hello you

A stranger unknown to me yet, I know of you. I lived in a world where I knew wonder was prevalent. A stranger and a mystery I have to see. When we meet our physical will need no introductions, my soul will silently say "hello you".

## <u>Plagued Air</u>

What is this plague that comes from the air? Consuming breaths of air, leaving us unaware? The wind the most obvious, the source concealed.

Where has it been sent from, has god sent it to restore us? Is it a punishment for living too fast and lasting too long? Consuming lives and taking for your own, dear lord how will we know when enough is enough?

While we live in fear we also live in reflection. As you take each soul back to your kingdom each soul you leave behind grows emotionally intelligent and faithfully aware. Your flock are coming together praying together, praying the words of hope, faith and love with the greatest of all being love.

## I place all my trust in thee

God is great, I place all my trust in thee. Why is it in our darkest times do we feel we wander alone. Words prayed day after day, week after week. "I place all my trust in thee" until one does not feel free. At times darkness takes over thoughts and faith with little rays to show the way, we lose the words that we used to say. Before the darkness completes into blackness we say the words "I place all my trust in thee" and from there we then begin again to see.

## <u>The faith is still there</u>

Friends unite on a different sight. Streets quiet, some empty, almost apocalyptic, shops closed, schools dormant, churches without their faith goers. Faith is still there you can feel it in the air.

Love is in abundance, the streets go quiet and still, the world retreating to their place of home. Love expressed through a thought and a prayer, the faith is still there. Schools and scholars alike turning to other frequencies to help moral and social instruction in a social distant happening.

Faith is still there it's in the air, people still care. Our churches empty, no place of worship so we worship everywhere. The good is in us, the faith is still there we move forward and continue to care.

## <u>Intelligent is not smart</u>

Intellect does not resonate smart. To be smart is to be without the formal education but still know you have many an education to offer. The man with the offering of what he is without the formal education and gives this freely is the man who lives happier and freer than the educated ego.

The educated ego believes the skills they have to offer are worth your pennies. These men stand behind podiums taking advice from more intellect who in turn demand more of your pennies and give back so little to the uneducated.

Why does it take such an educated man with an ego which demands financial gain need so many advisories behind him? Where the uneducated educates for free.

## Speak for yourself

When we read out our own words we talk with confidence.

It's when we read other peoples words we stumble. Continue speaking for oneself.

## The Introvert

Silence can say many things. Choose your silence wisely. The introverted and quiet that you are is perceived as no ambition, drive, or passion. This is what one may see.

The introvert stays silent working on his craft, should we consider the introvert without talent or skills, the introverted are thought to be soft and unchallenging.

The introverted do not need to be harsh or difficult. The introverted have logic and reason.

The introverted have given you presidency, communications, movies and technology. Be an introvert in an extrovert world and silently watch your succession come alive. No need for a stage when you have the worlds attention.

## Avoid dis-ease

Protect yourself, protect your mind, your body, your soul. Dis-ease of the mind, body and soul causes disease in the mind, body and soul. Refuse to accept what is unacceptable.

Dis-engage from the negative and emotionally controlling dis- ease kind. I am kind to my mind, I avoid dis-ease in my life and avoid disease in my body. I radiate positivity because I am so much more than that what the world reiterates, frustrates and communicates. Choose what you let in, bring your mind body and soul to ease and avoid dis-ease and disease.

## <u>Give Happiness</u>

Each life feeding off each life. When they are happy, you are happy.

When they are sad, you are sad for them.

Life's energy feeds into life's surroundings.

Be happy when they are happy, be happy when they are sad,

Their energy won't be able to avoid your energy,

Give your happiness to ease their sadness.

## **I look healthy**

I look healthy, I appear healthy, I don't act healthy, I don't think healthy. I construct my own destruction to avoid the unavoidable. I'm not healthy, I don't feel healthy. I need to talk to help me get healthy.

## The negative opinion

Listen to the negativity then thank them for their opinion, then disregard it in your head and continue on doing as you do. Don't let someone else's life learnt lesson of holding back, hold you back, who are they to taint your whole view on the progression of moving forward?

## <u>The heart smiles</u>

Every moment of today was a joy. I tripped but I didn't fall. I cried, but from laughter. I had a fight but it was about paying for a coffee bill. I smiled all day from things we normally associate with a frown. Not all trips, tears and fights hurt the heart. Some make it smile and feel an abundance of joy.

## Fly despite the weight

You can't do this her head said, you shouldn't feel this her heart whispered, you aren't ready her legs shook with weight. Then she did what her head told her she shouldn't, and felt what her heart whispered she shouldn't and she flew when the legs weren't ready.

We were always a step ahead, it's the self-doubt that keeps us a step behind. Step ahead, do what you couldn't, feel what you shouldn't and fly despite the weight you think you feel.

## **Step back for the mind**

I stepped back for my health. The pressure from the man and getting nowhere feeling useless, stupid yet busy and under pressure, getting nowhere but never stopping an endless cycle with no desired or directed outcome.

Then I stop!

Stepping back for your health is not admitting defeat. Take a seat, find your feet. When you're ready take your step forward into the old direction you missed with clarity or the new direction you find seeking clarity.

## It begins where it ends

It begins again where it ends. You will begin things and end things until you find the right things. You are not finished at each ending. Each ending is providing you with a new beginning. Cultivate the world start, stop, and end and begin again, when you find that thing that runs through your veins, you will have no desire to start again, just finish and begin your love again.

## If love didn't grow

If love didn't grow then there was no love lost when you let it go,

Give up the loveless mundane you are trying to gain for something that will never be in your vein.

## The start of the future

I made a decision today that today will be the start of my tomorrow and tomorrow will be the start of my future. Put your plan in place today and move forward tomorrow.

Reach the destination you were destined to reach. For our tomorrows are not promised. Do today what you would be proud to leave behind in the tomorrows you will never see?

## I am rich

I am not rich, yet I ate this morning. I was thirsty so I drank from my tap. It is not summer, yet I have heat to see me through a cold day. I said I was not rich, yet I ate today. I quenched my thirst from my own tap. I pressed a button and went from cold to warm. I am rich to those who do not have that luxury. The price of gratitude is free to give it to the things you are so lucky to have.

## No closed doors

I prepare tonight for tomorrow. And tomorrow I prepare for what is to come. Because I prepare I cannot fail, come what may I'm prepared for all outcomes. I am blessed either way. Learn from the fail or rejoice in my succession, there are no negatives just desired outcomes, no closed doors, just ones we haven't learnt to open YET!

# Dare to lead (your life)

The life you lead, dare to lead it. The life you lead is one constructed by you, thought out by you, your talents, your attitude your greatness. Execute the greatness in you, live what feels true. No not me, it's not true I can't do. But you already do, do that thing you do.

You do have the talent in you. If one was to think about how another should lead their life, one would point out only the great, the talent the awe one has for another.

Awe and amaze yourself, you must find great belief in you before you can show others how you do that thing you do. Once you find the awe you deserve in yourself, unleash to the world and peers you peer to.

See how the awe you have for another is what another has an awe for you.

## **Opportunity knocks**

Opportunity knocked, knock back, let it know you are there. It's OK to be scared to open the door just don't ignore it. Knock back, take a split second think on the spot. Knock back let opportunity know you heard the knock. Let them know your registering, when you've had your spilt second, when you know they are listening, open the door and say thank you. Thank you for knocking, thank you for receiving my knock and thank you for giving me my split second to realise how lucky I am.

## Thinking our thoughts

We think about our thoughts more than we ought. We think on our thoughts and struggle to know what we are thinking. Thinking clouds the mind but a thought can clear your head. Patience about our thinking. Allowing a thought to come through, can see YOU through.

Reflect on the thought, make true what you see. The thinking you thought can make a difference, share in what you see from the thinking that was just a thought.

## An idea

Thoughts, feelings, ideas of ideals come flooding through when it's just you, take note. Thoughts become realities, feelings becoming overwhelming and an idea can take you anywhere.

## **Music connection**

When someone wants to know you tell them of the songs you listened to when you were at a troublesome time. If they understand it, they get you, if they want to listen they want to know you. If they have no interest, then dance alone. Dance with those who want to understand your rhythm, if music is anything it is the rhythm of the soul.

## <u>Leave a legacy</u>

When you find the world not to your liking improve it, enlighten it, add to it, give a piece of yourself to it.

Leave a legacy of a song, of a story, of a poem, a painting, look to the world for inspiration, show your admiration, show appreciation then feel the appreciation others have for you.

Feel the beauty the world has to offer and express it in your own being, you don't lack inspiration and appreciation it is present in everything you see, and do.

## Swinging ropes

Life has been set up for you. You succeed in the new ventures, that was set up for you. Those ventures come to an end, that was set up for you. While jobless you learn resilience in finding new work. While finding new work you develop new skills, that was set up for you.

There are no failings in the fails, or losses in lost directions, simply new experiences and new paths, which were set up for you. You cannot fail or lose your true north when life has been set up for you. When life dangles swinging ropes, the ropes you chose to swing on were meant for you.

## Similarities in words

As I read one thing, I then read another. While some words become repetitive, I would also say life has different versions of everything. Words may repeat. Visions, delivery and ideas are unique. Similarities allows one to see they are not alone in their thinking's. It's how you present and deliver defines the message you want to say.

## <u>Dance</u>

Dance as though no one is watching, dance as though your soul demands it, wide arms, extended legs, full embrace of ones love of movement.

## **<u>Losing weight is easy they said</u>**

Losing weight is easy they said, as they said it from bed, eating chocolate spread. I looked at their heads. Lollipop in size and to my surprise they didn't even exercise.

We've good genes they said as they stepped out of bed and grabbed a loaf of bread. There I was thinking I'd love some ginger bread. Then I looked at my jeans size 12 it would seem, not all that extreme.

What could it mean to exercise to the extreme? Would it give me some pride? Would it give me a better stride? Would it make me a better bride should I ever wed?

I don't think I'll bother doing the shred I too love chocolate spread. A lollipop head I do not suit, so I think I will avoid the fruit.

Losing weight is easy they said words coming from their lollipop sized head.

Little did I know they didn't need to do the shred, they were allergic to bread, they had a side effect instead.

Terrible I know but when they had to go they had to go!

Maybe avoiding the bread and doing the shred will make me become a thoroughbred without the lollipop head. OK. Let's get back on the trend and work for that bread. Losing weight is easy they said.

Never again will I trust a lollipop head eating chocolate spread on bread from a bed.

## <u>Stained pages</u>

Stained pages, turned down corners, scruffy edges, worn out prints, those are the books I want to read, they have character, they have lived they have passed through many hands they have been read many times, they have enlightened and caused ripple effects in the lives of those who have read them. They are classics, they are favourites they are someone's place to revisit when they have nowhere to go. They are the great escape.

## People maketh the place

"The people maketh the place. The warm welcomes, the friendly hellos, the heartfelt good byes, the laughing till you cry's, the can I help, here have a brew. People maketh the place.

The concert streets, the cold and mostly wet ground, puddled most of the year round. Streets filled with the grey clouds but oh my, wait until you hear the sounds. Walk down any street and you will hear a hello, how are you doing, what's the craic.

Walk into any pub and be welcomed like one of their own. Who are you, and where do you come from? Do you want a drink, let's sing a song. Oh what a place to come from, the home town of Derry. The people maketh the place. "

## <u>Humbled</u>

Thank you and humble are one of the same. Thank you for reading. I'm humbled you hear me. You don't have to hear the words spoken to hear a voice.

Thank you.

Printed in Great Britain
by Amazon